D1709990

CountryMusic ★ Stars
JULIANNE HOUGH

By Aife Franke

Gareth Stevens
Publishing

Please visit our Web site, www.garethstevens.com. For a free color catalog of all our high-quality books, call toll free 1-800-542-2595 or fax 1-877-542-2596.

Library of Congress Cataloging-in-Publication Data

Franke, Aife.
 Julianne Hough / Aife Franke.
    p. cm. -- (Country music stars)
 Includes index.
 ISBN 978-1-4339-3933-4 (pbk.)
 ISBN 978-1-4339-3934-1 (6-pack)
 ISBN 978-1-4339-3932-7 (library binding)
 1. Hough, Julianne, 1988---Juvenile literature. 2. Singers--United States--Biography--
Juvenile literature. 3. Country musicians--United States--Biography--Juvenile literature.
 I. Title.
 ML3930.H69F73 2010
 782.421642092 la B--dc22
                            2010005883

First Edition

Published in 2011 by
Gareth Stevens Publishing
111 East 14th Street, Suite 349
New York, NY 10003

Copyright © 2011 Gareth Stevens Publishing

Designer: Haley W. Harasymiw
Editor: Therese Shea

Photo credits: Cover background Shutterstock.com; cover (Julianne Hough), pp. 1, 5, 9
Jason Merritt/Getty Images; pp. 7, 29 Ethan Miller/Getty Images; p. 11 Kevin Winter/
Getty Images; p. 13 Michael Buckner/Getty Images; p. 15 Ryan Miller/Getty Images;
pp. 17, 27 Rick Diamond/Getty Images; pp. 19, 23 Charley Gallay/Getty Images; pp.
21, 25 Frederick M. Brown/Getty Images.

Printed in the United States of America

CPSIA compliance information: Batch #CS10GS: For further information contact Gareth Stevens, New York, New York at 1-800-542-2595.

CONTENTS

TONS OF TALENT

Julianne Hough has lots of talent. She sings, dances, and acts!

Julianne became famous as a dancer.

However, she always wanted to be a

country music singer.

GROWING UP DANCING

Julianne was born on July 20, 1988.

She grew up in Utah.

9

Julianne has three sisters and a brother. Her brother, Derek, is a dance star, too.

Derek Hough

When Julianne was 10 years old, she moved away from her family. She studied dance in London, England.

13

Julianne trained long hours. She won several dance competitions. She also sang in a band called 2B1G.

FOLLOWING HER DREAM

Five years later, Julianne moved back to the United States. She wanted to start a music career.

17

Julianne moved to California when she was 18. She began dancing on a TV show. It was called *Dancing with the Stars.*

Julianne also began making trips to Nashville, Tennessee. She worked on her singing career there.

21

A BIG YEAR

In May 2007, Julianne and speed skater Apolo Ohno won *Dancing with the Stars*! Her first song came out that month, too.

Apolo Ohno

In November 2007, Julianne won *Dancing with the Stars* for a second time. Her partner was race-car driver Hélio Castroneves.

Hélio Castroneves

TIME TO SING

Julianne's first album came out in 2008. She called it *Julianne Hough*. It was number one on the country music charts.

Julianne's biggest hit was "That Song in My Head." She was named Best New Artist in 2009. She made her dream come true!

TIMELINE

1988   Julianne is born on July 20 in Utah.

1998   Julianne studies dance in London, England.

2003   Julianne moves back to the United States.

2007   Julianne wins *Dancing with the Stars* two times.

2008   Julianne's first album comes out.

2009   Julianne is named Best New Artist.

FOR MORE INFORMATION

Books:

Garofoli, Wendy. *Modern Dance*. Mankato, MN: Capstone
 Press, 2008.

Handyside, Chris. *Country*. Chicago, IL: Heinemann
 Library, 2006.

Web Sites:

CMT.com: Julianne Hough
www.cmt.com/artists/az/hough__julianne/artist.jhtml

Julianne Hough
www.juliannehough.com

Publisher's note to educators and parents: Our editors have carefully reviewed these Web sites to ensure that they are suitable for students. Many Web sites change frequently, however, and we cannot guarantee that a site's future contents will continue to meet our high standards of quality and educational value. Be advised that students should be closely supervised whenever they access the Internet.

GLOSSARY

career: a person's job

competition: an activity in which people try to do something better than others

partner: someone who dances with another person

INDEX